A Primary Source Guide to
MOROCCO

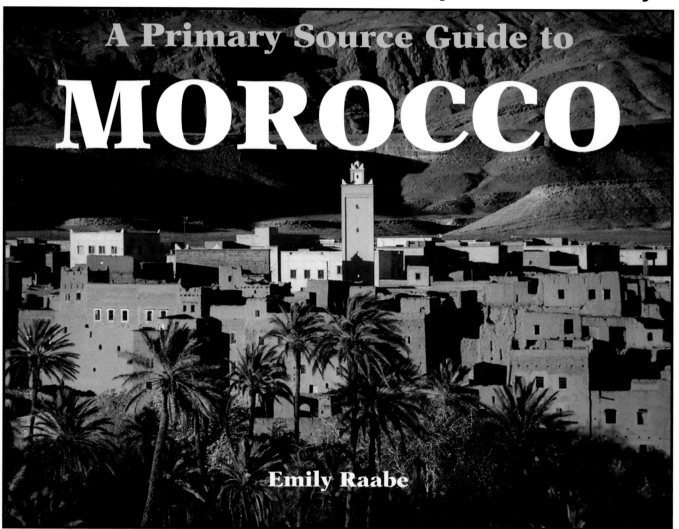

Emily Raabe

The Rosen Publishing Group's

PowerKids Press™
PRIMARY SOURCE

New York

For Emma, for whom the world has just begun

Published in 2005 by The Rosen Publishing Group, Inc.
29 East 21st Street, New York, NY 10010

First Edition

Editor: Rachel O'Connor
Book Design: Haley Wilson
Layout Design: Nick Sciacca
Photo Researcher: Adriana Skura

Photo Credits: Cover Image © Mark Daffey/Lonely Planet Images; p. 4 © 2002 Geoatlas, pp. 4 (inset), 6, 18 © Yann Arthus-Bertrand/Corbis; p. 8 © Owen Franken/Corbis; pp. 10, 18 (inset) © Carl & Ann Purcell/Corbis, (inset) © AFP/Corbis; p. 12 © Sean Sparague/The Image Works; p. 14 © Richard Bickel/Corbis; p. 16 © Nik Wheeler/Corbis. (inset) © Corbis; p. 20 © Robert Patrick/Corbis Sygma.

Library of Congress Cataloging-in-Publication Data

Raabe, Emily.
A primary source guide to Morocco / Emily Raabe—1st ed.
     v. cm. — (Countries of the world, a primary source journey)
Includes bibliographical references and index.
Contents: Morocco—Ocean and deserts—The Berbers—Sultans and kings—Morocco's economy—Berbers and Arabs—Islam—Morocco's cities—Celebrations and feasts.
ISBN 1-4042-2755-5 (library binding)
1. Morocco—Juvenile literature. [1. Morocco.] I. Title. II. Series.
DT305.R32 2005
964—dc22

                                    2003020974

Manufactured in the United States of America

Contents

PORTUGAL

SPAIN

MEDITERRANEAN SEA

STRAIT OF
GIBRALTAR

■ Rabat

TUNISIA

MOROCCO

ALGERIA

LIBYA

WESTERN
SAHARA

MAURITANIA

MALI

NIGER

CHAD

SENEGAL

GAMBIA

GUINEA-BISSAU

GUINEA

BURKINA
FASO

TOGO

BENIN

NIGERIA

SIERRA LEONE

CÔTE
D'IVOIRE

GHANA

CAMEROON

CENTRAL
AFRICAN
REPUBLIC

LIBERIA

4

*ATLANTIC
OCEAN*

EQUAT.
GUINEA

GABON

CONGO

Morocco

Morocco lies at the edge of North Africa, only 8 miles (13 km) across the **Strait** of Gibraltar from Spain. Morocco has an area of 274,461 square miles (710,851 sq km), which is slightly larger than the state of California. Morocco is bordered to the west by the Atlantic Ocean and to the north by the Mediterranean Sea. The country of Algeria lies on the eastern and southern borders of Morocco, and Mauritania is just south of Morocco, where the Western Sahara begins. The Sahara is a large desert in North Africa. The population of Morocco is about 31,689,265 people. Its capital city is Rabat, located on the northwestern coast.

◀ This map shows part of Africa, with Morocco on the very northwestern edge. The Strait of Gibraltar connects the Atlantic Ocean to the Mediterranean Sea. *Inset:* The capital city of Rabat can be found on Morocco's northwestern coast.

6

Geography and Climate

Morocco has a chain of mountains called the Atlas, which runs for 473 miles (761 km) down the center of the country. The Atlas Mountains are actually made up of three mountain ranges. These are the Middle Atlas range in the north, the High Atlas in the center of the country, and the Anti-Atlas range in the south. The weather to the west of the Atlas, near the ocean, is pleasant. The area has hot summers, with **temperatures** around 71°F (22°C), and wet, mild winters. Central Morocco, which is mountainous, gets thunderstorms in the summer and snow in the winter, with the temperature sometimes falling below 32°F (0°C). The eastern region of Morocco is very hot and dry.

◀ Morocco is a mountainous country. The highest mountain in the Atlas Mountains is Mount Toubkal. It stands at 13,665 feet (4,165 m) in the High Atlas range.

Early Morocco

The history of Morocco is one of battles, **invasions**, **sultans**, and kings. One of the earliest groups of people to live in what is now Morocco were the Berbers. The Berbers have lived in Morocco for thousands of years. No one knows where they came from. There were many Berber tribes, but the most powerful tribes were the Masmoudas, the Sanhajas, and the Zenata. These three tribes fought each other all the time to gain power. In the 600s and the 700s, **Arabs** from east of Morocco came to Morocco and **converted** the tribes to **Islam**. Even after they converted to Islam, the three tribes continued to fight. During the sixteenth and the seventeenth centuries, there were many battles between the Berber tribes.

Berbers in Morocco still live in tribes. They make up about half of Morocco's population. Pictured here is a Berber woman with her child.

The Moroccan King

By the 1900s, other countries had become interested in Morocco, and, by 1912, France and Spain had taken control of Morocco. Their rule lasted until 1956, when both countries agreed to give up their claims to Morocco. After many years of tribal wars, Morocco was a free country. Today Morocco is a **constitutional monarchy**. This means it has a government with a constitution and a king. The king hands his power down to his children. The king of Morocco is very powerful. He has the power to change laws or even to get rid of the government and rule by himself. The king is also the **religious** head of state in Morocco, which means he is in charge of Islam in the country.

Shown here is the gate of the Royal Palace in Rabat. *Inset:* Muhammad VI became king of Morocco following the death of his father King Hassan II in 1999.

12

Morocco's Economy

Morocco's **economy** is getting stronger all the time, although there is high **unemployment**. At least one-fifth of Moroccans, and perhaps more, are unemployed. The government of Morocco has been working hard since the 1980s to address this, but it remains a problem. Morocco's economy depends mostly on exporting, or sending goods out of the country to other countries to be sold. Morocco exports crops such as figs, oranges, sugarcane, and dates to countries around the world, including the United States. Morocco's main **mineral resource** is phosphate, a mineral that is used to make fertilizer. Fertilizer is a product that helps plants to grow.

Since the 1930s, fishing has been a very important industry, or business, in Morocco. Today more than 100,000 Moroccans are employed in the fishing industry. *Inset:* The unit of money that is used in Morocco is called the dirham.

14

The People

Most Moroccans are the **descendants** of either Arabs or Berbers. Arabic is the language spoken in the cities and the western coast of Morocco. The Berber language is still spoken in the mountains and eastern deserts. Many Moroccans also speak Spanish and French. Music is an important part of Moroccan life in both Berber villages and modern cities. Moroccan music is played on instruments such as the *bendir* drum, a round drum covered in cowhide, and the *rebab*, a **fiddle** with one string. Another important part of Moroccan life is the souk, or outdoor market. People buy and sell goods there. Souks often have storytellers, snake charmers, and singers.

◄ Morocco is famous for its beautiful, handmade carpets that are often sold in souks, or markets. Here carpets are on sale in a busy souk in Marrakech.

Islam

Ninety-nine percent of Moroccans are Muslims. This means that they practice Islam as their religion. Islam follows the teachings of Muhammad, a man who lived in the Arabian town of Mecca and died in A.D. 632. Muhammad's ideas are written down in a book called the Koran. Muslim Moroccans must pray five times each day. They must also visit the town of Mecca at least once in their lifetime. **Ramadan** is an important Muslim holiday. It lasts the entire ninth month of the Muslim calendar every year. During the month of Ramadan, Muslims must fast, or go without food, during daylight hours. This fasting can be very hard, but there are feasts and **celebrations** at the end of Ramadan.

◀ The places where Muslims pray are called mosques. Shown is the Karaouyine Mosque in Fès, the largest mosque in North Africa. *Inset:* Pictured are pages from the Koran that was made for the Sultan of Morocco in the eighteenth century.

18

Morocco's Capital Cities

Over the centuries, four different cities have served as Morocco's capital. These are Rabat, Fès, Marrakech, and Meknès. Rabat has been the capital of Morocco since 1913. This beautiful city lies along the coast of the Atlantic. Fès, lying northeast of Rabat, is the oldest of these four cities. It was founded in A.D. 808 and was Morocco's capital city in the 1200s. Marrakech, an eleventh-century capital city, lies in central Morocco. It was built by nomads from the Sahara. Nomads are people who move from place to place. Meknès, Morocco's capital city in the 1600s, was built on a **plateau** in the Middle Atlas Mountains. Meknès was also a military base in the 1600s. More than 25 miles (40 km) of thick walls surround Meknès!

This is a view of the city of Meknès. Notice the wall that surrounds it. *Inset:* The Bou Regreg River flows through Morocco's present-day capital, Rabat.

Celebrations and Feasts

The Moroccan people love celebrations, from giant holidays to small dinners with friends. A Moroccan wedding, for example, can last up to seven days and includes feasting, dancing, and singing every night. The end of the month of Ramadan marks another celebration for Moroccans, as does the two-day independence celebration every March 2 and 3. Moroccans are also known for welcoming people to their homes. A visit to a home in Morocco often means drinking at least three glasses of mint tea, and usually includes a meal as well. Even though it can sometimes be hard, life in Morocco is also full of beauty and celebration.

◀ Pictured here is a royal wedding that took place in 1994. Princess Lalla Hasnaa is being carried through the streets of Fès.

Morocco at a Glance

Population: 31,689,265

Capital City: Rabat

Largest City: Casablanca, population 2,940,623

Languages: Arabic and Berber. French is often used in business and government.

Official Name: The Kingdom of Morocco

Government: Constitutional monarchy

Unit of money: Dirham

Land Area: 274,461 square miles (710,851 sq km)

Highest Point: Mount Toubkal, 13,665 feet (4,165 m)

Flag: Green five-pointed star on a red background. Green is the color of Islam. In 1915, the French added the star, which is an ancient sign known as the seal of Solomon. Red stands for the descendants of the Islamic founder Muhammad.

Glossary

Arabs (AR-ubz) Members of a group of people who live in southern Asia or northern Africa.

celebrations (seh-luh-BRAY-shunz) Activities to observe special times.

constitutional monarchy (kon-stih-TOO-shuh-nul MAH-nar-kee) A government in which a country has both a ruler and elected leaders.

converted (kun-VERT-ed) To be changed from one religious belief to another.

descendants (dih-SEN-dents) People born of a certain family or group.

economy (ih-KAH-nuh-mee) The way in which a country or a business manages its supplies and energy sources.

fiddle (FIH-dul) A stringed musical instrument.

invasions (in-VAY-zhunz) Attacks in which armies take over a place.

Islam (IS-lom) A faith based on the teachings of Muhammad and the Koran.

mineral (MIH-ner-ul) A natural element that is not an animal, a plant, or another living thing.

plateau (pla-TOH) A broad, flat, high piece of land.

Ramadan (RAH-meh-don) The ninth month of the Muslim calendar, observed by daily fasting from sunrise to sunset.

religious (ree-LIH-jus) Faithful to a religion and its beliefs.

resource (REE-sors) A supply or source of energy or useful items.

strait (STRAYT) A narrow waterway connecting two larger bodies of water.

sultans (SUL-tinz) Rulers of Muslim countries.

temperatures (TEM-pruh-cherz) How hot or cold things are.

unemployment (un-em-PLOY-mint) The state of being without a job.

Index

Primary Source List

Page 4 (inset). Walled Medina, Rabat. Circa 1993. Photograph by Yann Arthus-Bertrand.
Page 6. Mount Toubkal in the High Atlas. Circa 1993. Photograph by Yann Arthus-Bertrand.
Page 8. A Berber woman with her child. 1991. Photograph by Owen Franken.
Page 10. Gate of the Royal Palace in Rabat. July 1977. Photograph by Ann Purcell.
Page 10 (inset). King Muhammad VI during a visit to Dakhla in the Western Sahara. November 1, 2001. Photograph by Abkelhak Senna.
Page 14. Carpets on display at a market in Marrakech. February 1998. Photograph by Richard Bickel.
Page 16. The Karaouyine Mosque in Fès. Circa 1970s–1990s. Photograph by Nik Wheeler.
Page 16 (inset). The Cairo Koran, Maghribi Script, was created for the Sultan of Morocco. Eighteenth century.
Page 18. City walls surround Meknès. Circa 1993. Photograph by Yann Arthus-Bertrand.
Page 18 (inset). The Bou Regreg River in Rabat. 1991. Photograph by Carl Purcell.
Page 20. The marriage of Princess Lalla Hasnaa in Fès. September 8, 1994. Photograph by Patrick Robert.

Web Sites

Due to the changing nature of Internet links, PowerKids Press has developed an online list of Web sites related to the subject of this book. This site is updated regularly. Please use this link to access the list:

www.powerkidslinks.com/cwpsj/psmoro/